EVERYDAY BLESSED

To my mom, who dedicated her life to the word of God and who lived an exemplary life of faith in God.

Arvin Kaufman

I AM BLESSED. GOD BLESSES ME EVERYWHERE I GO. HE IS WITH ME ALL THE TIME.

my notes

DAY 1

―――――――――⸙―――――――――

SCRIPTURE STUDY

PSALM 5:12

For You, O Lord, will bless the righteous;
With favor You will surround him as with a
shield.

Declare

I AM FULLY BLESSED. THERE ARE NO LIMITS TO WHAT GOD IS ABLE TO DO IN MY LIFE.

my notes

SCRIPTURE STUDY

MATTHEW 19:26

But Jesus looked at them and said to them, "With men this is impossible, but with God all things are possible."

GOD BLESSES ME ABUNDANTLY. HIS BLESSING IS ALL AROUND ME AND FLOWS TO OTHERS.

my notes

DAY 3

SCRIPTURE STUDY

GENESIS 12:2

I will make you a great nation;
I will bless you
And make your name great;
And you shall be a blessing.

ALL GOOD THINGS COME FROM GOD. I WILL PRAISE HIM FOREVER AND EVER.

my notes

DAY 4

―――――∘⟨⟩⟨⟩∘―――――

Scripture Study

PSALM 103:1-5

Bless the Lord, O my soul;
And all that is within me, bless His holy name!
Bless the Lord, O my soul,
And forget not all His benefits:
Who forgives all your iniquities,
Who heals all your diseases,
Who redeems your life from destruction,
Who crowns you with lovingkindness and
tender mercies,
Who satisfies your mouth with good things,
So that your youth is renewed like the eagle's.

―――――∘⟨⟩⟨⟩∘―――――

I AM DAILY BLESSED WITH JOY FROM THE PRESENCE OF THE LORD.

my notes

DAY 5

SCRIPTURE STUDY

PSALM 21:6

For You have made him most blessed forever;
You have made him exceedingly glad with
Your presence.

GOD SO LOVES ME.

my notes

DAY 6

SCRIPTURE STUDY

JOHN 3:16

For God so loved the world that He gave His only begotten Son, that whoever believes in Him should not perish but have everlasting life.

GOD CREATED ME TO BE DISTINGUISHED, TO STAND OUT. I AM BLESSED, A CLASS APART.

my notes

DAY 7

SCRIPTURE STUDY

PSALM 8:5-6

For You have made him a little
lower than the angels,
And You have crowned him
with glory and honor.
You have made him to have
dominion over the works of Your hands;
You have put all things under his feet,

Declare

I AM GOD'S SPECIAL TREASURE. MADE BY GOD, FASHIONED TO LOOK LIKE HIM AND BE LIKE HIM WITH HONOR AND RESPECT.

my notes

DAY 8

SCRIPTURE STUDY

EPHESIANS 4:23-24

..and be renewed in the spirit of your mind, and that you put on the new man which was created according to God, in true righteousness and holiness.

Declare

JESUS IS IN ME. GOD LOVES ME JUST AS MUCH AS HE LOVES JESUS.

my notes

DAY 9

SCRIPTURE STUDY

JOHN 17:23

I in them, and You in Me; that they may be made perfect in one, and that the world may know that You have sent Me, and have loved them as You have loved Me.

I AM THE OBJECT OF GOD'S AFFECTION. GOD BLESSES ME AND MAKES HIS FACE TO SHINE ON ME.

my notes

DAY 10

SCRIPTURE STUDY

NUMBERS 6:22-26

"The Lord bless you and keep you;
The Lord make His face shine upon you,
And be gracious to you;
The Lord lift up His countenance upon you,
And give you peace."

Declare

IN THE NAME OF JESUS I APPROACH THE FATHER AND I BELIEVE THAT I RECEIVE ANYTHING THAT I ASK FOR.

my notes

DAY 11

SCRIPTURE STUDY

JOHN 16:24

Most assuredly, I say to you,
whatever you ask the Father in My name He
will give you.
Until now you have asked nothing in My
name. Ask, and you will receive, that your joy
may be full.

Declare

GOD CROWNS MY LIFE WITH FAVOR, GOOD THINGS OVERFLOW EVERYWHERE AROUND ME.

my notes

DAY 12

SCRIPTURE STUDY

PSALM 23:5-6

You prepare a table before me in the
presence of my enemies;
You anoint my head with oil;
My cup runs over.
Surely goodness and mercy shall follow me
All the days of my life;
And I will dwell in the house of the Lord
Forever.

―――⦿―――

THE SAME BLESSING ABRAHAM HAD ON HIS LIFE IS NOW ON MINE TOO. THANK YOU, JESUS.

my notes

SCRIPTURE STUDY

GALATIANS 3:29

And if you are Christ's, then you are Abraham's seed, and heirs according to the promise.

THE LORD'S GOODNESS, MERCY AND LOVE ARE FOREVER.

my notes

DAY 14

SCRIPTURE STUDY

PSALM 136

Oh, give thanks to the Lord, for He is good!
For His mercy endures forever.
Oh, give thanks to the God of gods!
For His mercy endures forever.
Oh, give thanks to the Lord of lords!
For His mercy endures forever:

Declare

I HAVE PEACE, RIGHT STANDING, LEGAL ACCESS AND FAVOR WITH GOD.

my notes

SCRIPTURE STUDY

ROMANS 5:1

Therefore, having been justified by faith,
we have peace with God
through our Lord Jesus Christ

I WAKE UP EXPECTING GOD'S GOODNESS AND MERCY AND DECLARING IT SO.

my notes

DAY 16

SCRIPTURE STUDY

PSALM 27

I would have lost heart,
unless I had believed
That I would see the goodness of the Lord
In the land of the living.

I LIVE A VICTORIOUS LIFE BECAUSE THE FAVOR OF GOD IS ON MY LIFE.

my notes

DAY 17

SCRIPTURE STUDY

PSALM 41:11

By this I know that You
are well pleased with me,
Because my enemy
does not triumph over me.

THE LORD KNOWS ME BY NAME, HE IS PLEASED WITH ME AND I HAVE FOUND FAVOR WITH HIM.

my notes

DAY 18

───────⚬───────

SCRIPTURE STUDY

EXODUS 33:14

And He said, "My Presence will go with you,
and I will give you rest."

───────⚬───────

Declare

I FEAR NOT, THE LORD FIGHTS FOR ME.

my notes

EXODUS 14:13

And Moses said to the people,
"Do not be afraid. Stand still, and see the salvation of the Lord, which He will accomplish for you today. For the Egyptians whom you see today, you shall see again no more forever.

Declare

THE LORD LOVES ME UNCONDITIONALLY AND WITHHOLDS NOTHING FROM ME.

my notes

SCRIPTURE STUDY

PSALM 68:19

Blessed be the Lord,
Who daily loads us with benefits,
The God of our salvation! Selah

Declare

THE LORD IS GOOD, THIS I BELIEVE.

my notes

DAY 21

JOHN 11:40

Jesus said to her,
"Did I not say to you that if you would believe
you would see the glory of God?"

THE LORD'S ANGELS GUARD AND PROTECT ME EVERYWHERE I GO.

my notes

DAY 22

SCRIPTURE STUDY

PSALM 91:10-12

No evil shall befall you,
Nor shall any plague come near your dwelling;
For He shall give His angels charge over you,
To keep you in all your ways.
In their hands they shall bear you up,
Lest you dash your foot against a stone.

THE LORD SHOWS ME HIS GLORY AND GOODNESS DAILY.

my notes

DAY 23

EXODUS 33:19

Then He said, "I will make all My goodness pass before you, and I will proclaim the name of the Lord before you.
I will be gracious to whom I will be gracious, and I will have compassion on whom I will have compassion."

Declare

I WALK WITH THE LORD AND HE HAS SO MANY GOOD THINGS IN STORE FOR ME.

my notes

DAY 24

SCRIPTURE STUDY

PSALM 31:19

Oh, how great is Your goodness,
Which You have laid up f
or those who fear You,
Which You have prepared
for those who trust in You
In the presence of the sons of men!

Declare

I PRAISE THE LORD ALWAYS FOR HIS GOODNESS.

my notes

DAY 25

—⟨∘⟩—

SCRIPTURE STUDY

PSALM 107:8

Oh, that men would give thanks to the Lord
for His goodness,
And for His wonderful works to the children of
men!

—⟨∘⟩—

Declare

I WILL PRAISE MY LORD; ALL HIS PROMISES ARE TRUE AND NOTHING IS IMPOSSIBLE FOR HIM.

my notes

SCRIPTURE STUDY

GENESIS 18:14

Is anything too hard for the Lord?
At the appointed time I will return to you,
according to the time of life, and Sarah shall
have a son.

Declare

NOTHING COMPARES TO YOUR EVERLASTING GOODNESS OH LORD.

my notes

DAY 27

SCRIPTURE STUDY

PSALM 34:8

Oh, taste and see that the Lord is good;
Blessed is the man who trusts in Him!

Declare

THE LORD'S GREAT GOODNESS REACHES EVERYWHERE AND EVERYONE.

my notes

DAY 28

SCRIPTURE STUDY

PSALM 113:7-9

He raises the poor out of the dust,
And lifts the needy out of the ash heap,
That He may seat him with princes—
With the princes of His people.
He grants the barren woman a home,
Like a joyful mother of children.
Praise the Lord!

THE LORD IS WHERE MY HELP COMES FROM.

my notes

SCRIPTURE STUDY

PSALM 20:6-7

Now I know that the Lord saves His anointed;
He will answer him from His holy heaven
With the saving strength of His right hand.
Some trust in chariots, and some in horses;
But we will remember
the name of the Lord our God.

Declare

I CONFIDENTLY RELY ON THE LORD'S FRESH SUPPLY OF HIS GOODNESS DAILY.

my notes

DAY 30

SCRIPTURE STUDY

LAMENTATIONS 3:22-23

Through the Lord's mercies we are not
consumed,
Because His compassions fail not.
They are new every morning;
Great is Your faithfulness.

Declare

THE END OF ALL THINGS IS GOOD FOR HE LOVES ME AND CARES GREATLY CONCERNING ME.

my notes

DAY 31

PSALM 65:11

You crown the year with Your goodness,
And Your paths drip with abundance.

MY DECLARATIONS

1. I am blessed. God blesses me everywhere I go. He is with me all the time.

2. I am fully Blessed. There are no limits to what God is able to do in my life.

3. God blesses me abundantly. His blessing is all around me and flows to others.

4. All these good things come from God; I will praise him forever and ever.

5. I am daily blessed with joy from the presence of the Lord.

6. God so loves me.

7. God created me to be distinguished, to stand out. I am blessed, a class apart.

8. I am God's special treasure. Made by God, fashioned to look like him and be like him with honour and respect.

9. Jesus is in me. God loves me just as much as he loves Jesus.

10. I am the object of God's affection. God BLESSES me and makes His face to shine on me.

11. In the name of Jesus, I approach the Father and I believe that I receive anything that I ask for.

12. God crowns my life with favor, good things overflow everywhére around me.

13. The same Blessing Abraham had on his life is now on mine too. Thank you, Jesus.

14. The Lord's goodness, mercy and love are forever!

15. I have peace, right standing, legal access and favor with God.

Everyday Blessed

MY DECLARATIONS

16. I wake up expecting God's goodness and mercy and declaring it so.

17. I live a victorious life because the favor of God is on my life.

18. The Lord knows me by name, He is pleased with me and I have found favor with Him.

19. I fear not, The Lord fights for me.

20. The Lord loves me unconditionally and withholds nothing from me.

21. The Lord is good, this I believe.

22. The Lord's angels guard and protect me everywhere I go.

23. The Lord shows me His glory and goodness daily.

24. I walk with the Lord and He has so many good things in store for me.

25. I praise the Lord always for His goodness.

26. I will praise my Lord; all His promises are true and nothing is impossible for Him.

27. Nothing compares to your everlasting goodness oh Lord.

28. The Lord's great goodness reaches everywhere and everyone.

29. The Lord is where my help comes from.

30. I confidently rely on the Lord's fresh supply of His goodness daily.

31. The end of all things is good for He loves me and cares greatly concerning me.

Everyday Blessed

DIARY
Journal your gratitude

DIARY

Journal your gratitude

www.ingramcontent.com/pod-product-compliance
Lightning Source LLC
Chambersburg PA
CBHW051212050326
40689CB00008B/1286